Creepy Creatures

Snails

Monica Hughes

Raintree

Chicago, Illinois

© 2004 Raintree
Published by Raintree, an imprint of Capstone Global Library, LLC.
Chicago, Illinois
Customer Service 888-363-4266
Visit our website at www.raintreelibrary.com

For information, address the publisher:
Raintree, 100 N. LaSalle, Suite 1200, Chicago, IL 60602

Printed and bound in the United States of America, North Mankato, Minnesota.
16 15 14
17 16 15

Library of Congress Cataloging-in-Publication Data:
Hughes, Monica.
   Snails / Monica Hughes.
       p. cm. -- (Creepy creatures)
Includes bibliographical references (p.   ).
Contents: Snails -- Looking for snails -- A snail's body -- A snail's
tentacles -- Snail trails -- Snail eggs -- Food for snails -- Snails in
danger -- Snails in winter -- Types of snails.
   ISBN 1-4109-0625-6 (lib. bdg. : hardcover) -- ISBN 1-4109-0651-5 (pbk.)
   ISBN 978-1-4109-0625-0 (lib. bdg. : hardcover) -- ISBN 978-1-4109-0651-9 (pbk.)
   1. Snails--Juvenile literature. [1. Snails.] I. Title. II. Series:
Hughes, Monica. Creepy creatures.
   QL430.4.H848 2003
   594'.3--dc21
                                    2003008289

Acknowledgments
The Publishers would like to thank the following for permission to reproduce photographs: p. 7 Heather
Angel; pp. 6, 21 Ardea: John Daniels, p. 19 Steve Hopkin, pp. 12, 22a, 22b, A Weaving; pp. 4/5, 17 BBC
NHU: Juan Manuel Borrero; p. 14 Bruce Coleman: Jane Burton; p. 22c Holt ; p. 16 Natural Visions:
Brian Rogers; p. 13 NHPA: Ant Photo Library, p. 11 Image quest 3D, p. 10 E.A Janes; pp. 15, 18 Oxford
Scientific Films: p. 20 K.G Vock; pp. 8, 9 Robert Harding Picture Library

Cover photograph reproduced with permission of Premaphotos/K.Preston-Mapham

Every effort has been made to contact copyright holders of any material reproduced in this book.
Any omissions will be rectified in subsequent printings if notice is given to the publishers.

Some words are shown in bold, **like this.** You can find out
what they mean by looking in the glossary on page 24.

112014
008579R

Contents

Snails

Snails are small animals that live outside.

shell

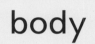

body

They have soft, slimy bodies and hard shells.

Kinds of Snails

There are many different kinds of snails.

Some snails live on land.

Other snails live in water.

Snail Bodies

A snail's body is called a **foot**.

foot

A snail can pull its
foot into its shell.

Snail Tentacles

Snails have four **tentacles** on their heads.

Two tentacles taste and smell.

eye tentacle

tasting and smelling tentacle

Two tentacles have eyes.

Snail Trails

Snails move very slowly.

They slide along on trails of slimy **mucus**.

Looking for Snails

Snails live in gardens.

You might find some in a flower pot.

You might find snails
in some leaves.

New Snails

New snails **hatch** from round, white eggs.

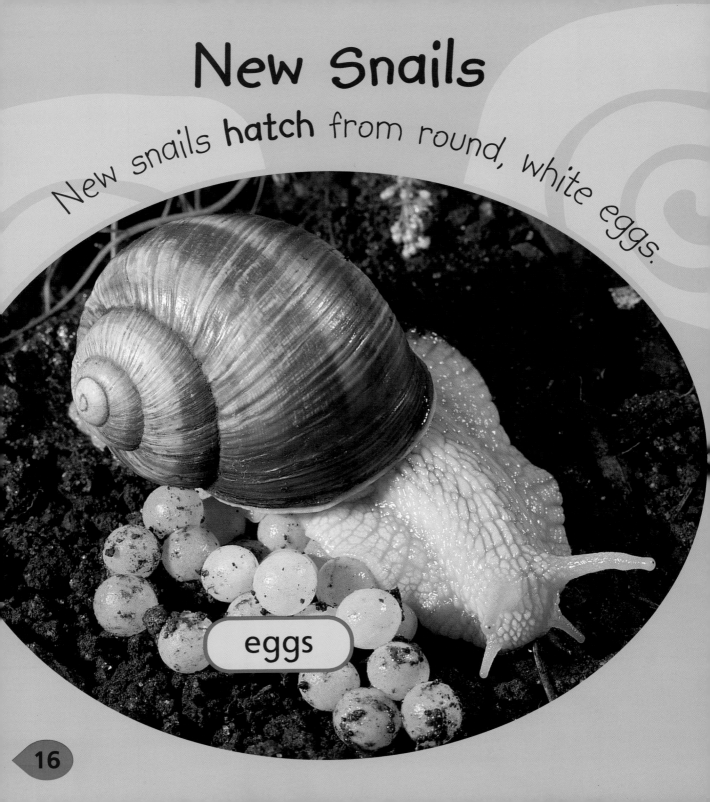

eggs

Baby snails are very small.
They have soft shells and bodies.

Food for Snails

Snails eat the leaves and flowers of dead plants.

They eat growing plants, too.
Snails can be garden pests.

Snails in Danger!

These snails are in danger.

They have pulled their bodies inside their shells.

foam

Snails can make foam, too.
Foam keeps snails safe
from **predators**.

Snails in Winter

Snails **hibernate** all winter.

They go inside their shells and close them with **mucus**.